Dog Training

Enhance Your Canine's Cognitive Abilities With This Compact Manual On Dogs' Iq Training And Assessment, Designed To Stimulate And Educate Your Young Dog's Mind

(A Comprehensive Manual On Acquiring, And Instructing A Robust Labradoodle)

Russell Caldwell

TABLE OF CONTENT

Acquiring Knowledge Of Typical Dog Behaviors 1

Concerning Treats 5

Clicker Instruction 18

Uncover The Clicker's Power 18

Taking Control Of Your Dog's Life 36

Recognize The Drives And Instincts Of The Dutch Shepherd 50

Educing Your Spanish 72

Transitioning From Watched To Unwatched Time 91

Bringing Your Dachshund Home 115

Part Iv Of The Four C's 1 144

Puppy Exercises That Take Less Than Ten Minutes 160

Acquiring Knowledge Of Typical Dog Behaviors

Recall that it's not always possible to interpret a dog's body language correctly. Since every dog differs from the next, they will all express themselves differently. By waving its tail joyfully, a dog may be trying to tell another dog that it is uneasy or uncomfortable. It is best to read a dog's body language rather than its breed, size, or outward look to determine whether or not it will bite. Remember that it is challenging to understand a dog's body language accurately, and proceed with caution when you are around unfamiliar dogs.

Monitor your dog to see if he routinely displays body language or gestures that convey his emotions. Until you can recall your dog's motions by heart, it's a good idea to record your observations in a diary.

Some dogs have curling Spitz-type tails, so you'll need to rely more on face and body postures to interpret what the dog's tail position might be trying to tell you. This will require a sharp eye. It is harder to read what breeds with dark coloring, flat features, and docked tails are attempting to say. Black-colored canines might have difficult-to-see facial emotions from a distance. Breeds with long hair, thick hair, or hair that covers up their facial features are causing more problems.

It will take some time to become adept at reading your dog's body language, but once you can quickly decipher your dog's intentions and feelings from his body language, you will have a stronger, longer-lasting bond. Pay attention to your dog's ears, eyes, lips, mouth, body postures, and tail movements. You will also improve at training and interacting with other people's dogs and your own. This is how you start learning to speak like a dog. This skill can only be acquired by studying canine communication, studying dogs, and having faith in your intuition. You can eventually learn the significance of your dog's messages using daily concentrated observations.

Do not be alarmed or overwhelmed by the procedure I have described because certain dogs' body language is simple to recognize and understand. As previous dog owners would tell you, you learn more about dogs' behaviors the more time you spend with them. You'll eventually learn more about how dogs behave, and as a result, you'll notice little adjustments in how you interact with all canines. The procedure is fun because you are spending time with your German Shepherd. Every dog trainer is always improving their dog's language abilities.

Concerning Treats

Dog owners can make treats from a wide variety of ingredients. Treats should always be roughly the size of a corn kernel. This makes them simple to remove from treat pouches while maintaining a flavor that will make your dog want to eat them.

A dog only needs a hint of taste to be engaged. The kernel size can be quickly consumed and ingested, so it won't interfere with the training. A reward should not be utilized as a meal or snack but rather as a brief taste used to entice and reinforce behavior.

Because your puppy is the best dog in the world, you are training him or her, and things are going well. As a result, you should be careful to give your dog the proper kinds of rewards. Treating your dog is simple as long as you avoid foods and beverages bad for them, such as chocolate, coffee, tea, avocados, onions, garlic, macadamia nuts, peaches, plums, pits, and seeds.

Treats must be of a better caliber and something your dog wants when you're out in the great outdoors with lots of distractions. Trainers refer to it as a higher-value treat because your dog should be rewarded for taking a break from their current activity. Cheese cubes, dried meats, or cooked meats might be a high-value reward for your dog.

Keep a range of snacks on hand to ensure that the types of rewards are varied. When your puppy turns his nose up at a treat because he has become weary of it or thinks it is less valuable than his hobbies, nothing worse can happen during training.

Kinds of Candy

Dogs can safely consume most fruits and vegetables, cooked or raw meats chopped up, yogurt, peanut butter, kibble, and whatever else you find your dogs enjoy. Just ensure it's healthy for them, especially their digestive systems. Note that not every food made for humans is suitable for dogs. When introducing new reward ideas to your dog, please examine and read about your dog's stools.

How often have you heard a friend or relative rave about a strange dish their dog adores? Dogs enjoy a huge range of foods, but not everything they perceive as desirable is healthy. Dog training is not complicated, but it requires some reading, common sense, and observation of your dog's behavior after consuming a treat.

Many enjoy making their goodies, and that's perfectly acceptable as long as you follow the guidelines we just discussed and pay attention to what you're adding while having fun in the kitchen. Keep in mind to look up and study the list of vegetables that dogs may and cannot eat, and be aware that seeds and pits can lead to intestinal problems, including the dreaded flatulence in dogs. Before cutting all fruits and vegetables into doggie-sized snacks, remove any seeds and pits and thoroughly clean them.

Check the ingredients on the treat box before you buy to be sure there are no dangerous chemicals, fillers, additions, colors, or other components. Your dog may not find certain human meals as appetizing as we do, and he will let you know. Most dogs enjoy eating meat, either raw or cooked. These snacks are perfect for focusing their attention on the desired area because of their small bite size.

Here are some suggestions for treats:

- Whole-grain cereals are a fantastic option. Cheerios without added sugar are one such example.

- Kibbles or dry meals. Place some in a paper bag and add some bacon or similar pork products to increase the scent. Dogs are completely captivated by delicious scents.

- Beef jerky without a lot of flavor or pepper added.

- Apple slices, carrots, and some dogs even like melons.

- Cubed meats that are simple to prepare at home and are not overly processed or salted. Cooked leftovers can be used.

- Cheese that has been shredded, diced, or strung. Dogs adore cheese!

- Spray cheese, cream cheese, or peanut butter. Reward your dog with a tiny treat to lick for each correct behavior. These are useful for teaching puppies to go outdoors for potty breaks after they ring a bell.

- Dogs love baby food meat items, even though they don't seem particularly appetizing to us.

- Ice Cubes: proceed with caution if your dog has dental issues.

- Commercial dog treats are widely available; exercise caution while selecting one. Seek for products free of artificial coloring, byproducts, and preservatives. Remember to provide the nation of origin as well.

You do not want to teach your four-legged companion that begging is okay, so never feed or otherwise care for them from the dining room table. When giving out treats, stay away from the dinner table and places where people typically congregate to eat, like the BBQ.

The Time to Attend

Between meals is the ideal time to provide goodies to dogs. When scheduling your training sessions, remember that all goodies are less effective if given too soon before or right after meals. Have a high-value treat on hand in case you need to bring your dog back into the training session during the session.

A full dog will be less likely to want a treat reward than a little peckish one. Your dog will probably find training sessions more challenging and less successful if they are not hungry. For this reason, it's a good idea to use toys, play, or praise instead of only treats to reinforce positive behavior.

- Affection and attention are rewards in that they represent positive reinforcement that can be just as powerful as food. Treating a dog involves giving them attention, praise, and treats. Playing with them or spending quality time with their preferred rope toy works well, too. These goodies can be quite important while training your dog.

- Never reward your dog with a goodie without asking them to perform a task. Declare, "sit," and then give your dog the treat once they comply. This strengthens both their obedience and your instruction.

- Refrain from giving your dog attention while he is hyperactive, disoriented, and unfocused. This could be detrimental and perpetuate a bad habit that makes attracting your dog's attention difficult.

- They have an excellent sense of smell, so they will detect the presence of a delicious snack long before you do. Just keep it hidden. Give your dog the command and wait for them to comply before giving them the treat. Recall that while giving your dog treats, it's crucial to be kind and patient, but it's also crucial to hold off on giving them until they comply. While some dogs are naturally kind and always receive things from your hand gracefully, other dogs require considerable training to develop this quality. You can teach your dog to say "gentle!" when receiving treats if they like to grab them a little rough. Moving forward, maintain your firmness. Treats should only be given after being gently removed from your hand. If you resolve to do this, your dog will eventually cooperate if he wants the delicious treat.

Comparing Reward Dog Treatment and Bribery

My friend discussed bribing the other day for an action he had ordered. After considering it, I decided to make it clearer for my readers. Bribery is the practice of visibly presenting the food in advance to get the dog to obey a command or change a behavior. Giving your dog his favorite toy, treat, attention, or love after he obeys an order is called a reward.

Bribery can take many forms, such as holding a steak cube in front of your dog so they can see it before you call for them to come. Giving your dog a steak as a reward for following the command is a good idea. Never give instructions before displaying the treats.

Dogs that are bribed only obey you when they are offered food. The rewarded dog learns they can only get rewards for carrying out the desired behaviors. Introducing non-food things as rewards for training and treating also helps with this.

Clicker Instruction
Uncover The Clicker's Power

I'll use the clicker in the upcoming chapters to walk you through each training command step-by-step. You should utilize the clicker, and I highly recommend it. Once a command is ingrained into your dog's subconscious, clicker training is a very powerful tool for getting inside his head and teaching him to behave intuitively when given. Using a dog clicker that produces a clicking sound to teach your dog to associate a sound with a command and a reward if he obeys is the basic idea behind clicker training. Dogs pick up new skills quickly through conditioning, which is furthered by the clicker.

Things to Think About

The clicker is a teaching tool, which is the first thing to realize. It is not something you will require indefinitely. You can stop using the clicker after your dog understands what you want him to accomplish. While you own your dog, you won't need to keep it on you at all times unless you like the sound of a quick clicker when you walk alone. Everybody to their own.

Second, remember that there are other rewards you can give in addition to treats. They work incredibly well, especially during the first training of your American Akita. But more often than not, you can give him affection and praise, a toy, and only the occasional treat as a reward for excellent behavior after he understands your instructions. Change things up to keep him wondering and anticipating what he might get if he follows your instructions.

Lastly, calorie-dense dog treats are not necessary. Give your dog little snacks, such as a tiny piece of jerky or a kernel of corn, or any well-known, wholesome, and enhanced dog treats available on the market. For this reason, even if you treat him frequently enough, smaller snacks won't wear him out, encourage laziness, or lead him to acquire weight. Additionally, they fit easily in your pocket. If you want to take your dog for a walk, you can buy a dog treat pouch at your neighborhood pet store or on

Amazon for a small fee. Keep these candies hidden. For example, you give your dog the sit command to teach him how to sit. When he does, you pull the food or toy in your pocket and give it to him.

Stopping your American Akita during play and giving him a command is a good practice. Remove his toy and retain it. Apply a directive. Click when he completes the task, then return the toy to him.

The Clicker's Operation

The clicker operates by employing a technique called shaping in dog training. Shaping is the process of teaching your dog a desired command by using incremental steps. You mold his mentality by rewarding him every time he carries out a task the way you want. Additionally, you will extend the command duration in each succeeding shape. Your dog will eventually come to identify the clicking sound with being rewarded. He will discover that if he follows your instructions, he will hear a click and receive a reward. He will eventually become so well-conditioned that he won't require the treat or the clicker. He will simply follow your instructions. "What a Good Boy That Is!"

Why using a clicker is preferable to verbal cues like "Good" may be a question on your mind. This is so that your dog won't confuse the clicker's distinctive sound for anything else. The human voice can sound different at different times and tones, and many English words have similar demands. However, the click's sound and volume never change. It always does the same thing. We also adore training your American Akita consistently.

How Clicker Training Is Done

Purchase a clicker at Amazon.com. Next, apply it each time you teach your dog a new trick, behavior, or command. When he gets the command correct, use a click. Next, reward yourself.

Maintaining consistency is essential. When your dog obeys your commands, that is the precise moment to activate the clicker. You can utilize it when he follows your instructions or when he acts independently. Throughout training, use your clicker until your dog has mastered listening to you.

Teach your dog a command first. When teaching him to keep still, click and reward him only when he is motionless. You might have to force him to sit by pushing his body into the posture. After he settles in, you click and reward him. By doing this, you can teach him the desired behavior for whatever command or cue you give him.

You can also train him to link a desired behavior to reacting to a particular stimulus. You can use the clicker to teach him to remain silent when the mailman arrives. After he doesn't bark at the mailman, click and give him a gift.

When your American Akita does not perform the specified activity, never click or reward them. He will become confused if you do this. You should continue to be reliable, even though I use the word consistently. Teach him to anticipate praise and click solely for following your instructions.

You may be doing something incorrectly if your dog is not responding to clicker training. Perhaps you are misguiding him. Make an effort to teach him the cue or command more. Go over this again. Be more straightforward, explicit, and distraction-free in your communication.

Perhaps he is overly interested in eating and isn't listening to you because you give him too many sweets. In this instance, take a brief break. After around twenty minutes, resume your training. Change things up a little by giving out prizes other than candy. However, he may be unsatisfied with the incentive you offer. I advise against using sauerkraut; that's for a different kind of dog you might see in New York City.

Is he gobbling them down as if they are the last treats in the canine world, or is he nipping and spitting? Maybe your American Akita thinks it's not worth the work. In such a situation, substitute his preferred reward for the original one. Replace a toy that's not so popular with his favorite, or look for treats he truly enjoys. I'll never understand why my dog prefers one, but I know each dog has a favorite. And so will your American Akita. Finding out about their personalities is kind of sweet. This means that you are in for a real treat.

You may have solely taught your dog indoors. He believes the context is different now that you are in the open. Gradually introduce him to new and varied settings to help him learn that cues and commands are the same everywhere.

Trial and error is a part of the clicker training process. Think of this as a long-term collaboration with your close friend. Based on his answers, determine what you do and how you do it. Save what functions, discard what doesn't, and swap it out with what does. Point, Click, Treat.

Chapter 7: Making Your Service More Social Canine

Mixing Up Your Pet or Youngster

Increasing socializing is essential to prevent behavioral problems. Socialization is very important before the dog turns six months old, but it should also continue throughout the dog's life. Careful socialization plays a major role in preventing hostility and fearful behavior. Lack of socializing can lead to agitated behavior, yapping, shyness, and hostility. The earlier you begin socializing your dog, the better, but all mutts can be gradually introduced to unfamiliar, even frightening, situations and taught to appreciate them. Socialization is a process with profound roots. If, for example, your dog doesn't see any dogs for several months or even years, you would expect that when he finally sees them again, his behavior will be different around them.

The best way to get your dog to try something new or something he is wary of is:

- If he wears a rope, maintain your composure and positive attitude while keeping it free.

- Gradually reveal to him the things he fears without ever pushing him. Give him the option to withdraw if necessary as well.

- Give him credit for remaining silent or looking into the new situation.

Try to expose your dog to anything and every situation regularly; you may want him to be able to adjust to it peacefully in the future. Make enough progress slowly so your dog can enjoy the sessions easily. It will seem like a lot of work from the beginning, but the reward will be a well-mannered dog! These are only a few examples; they are not an exhaustive list:

- Meeting new people of all kinds, such as children, men, swarms, people with caps on, people who are disabled, and so on.

- Getting to know new dogs (due to disease risk, take your puppy only to areas with many dogs after four months).

Unless, of course, it's a well-run puppy kindergarten. For this, positive education courses are fantastic.

- Being around various animals as pets, such as horses, cats, or birds

- Show him how to maximize his argument.

- Riding in the car (be sure to use a certified container or dog safety belt to keep him under control for his safety).

- Being readied and cleaned in different ways, held, and contacted once everything was done.

- Going to the groomer, daycare, boarding pet hotel, and veterinarian's office.

- Being around strange objects and loud noises (such as an umbrella opening).

- Contact with vehicles, bicycles, skateboards, and joggers.

- Acclimating him to being ignored one after another for a few hours.

Reactive action: Keeping a safe distance from problems requires socialization and the creation of a respectable living environment. Try to picture every amazing thing that happens to people he should know is okay with us, like getting washed, walking on sidewalks, using vacuum cleaners, etc. Assert your dog that these things are not scary by introducing them little by little with toys, food, and praise.

Making arrangements for contact through planning is another major avoidance. You will be well on your way to resolving any future problems with the dog once you have demonstrated to him that you are in charge of all of his favorite things and that you will, whenever feasible, compensate for quiet behavior.

Maintain the dog in a healthy state for him. Regardless of whether his intelligence is being assessed or he gets adequate opportunities to interact with other dogs and people, consider the amount of activity he receives. Make sure he follows a healthy diet and that his well-being is maintained.

Allow him to experience the confidence from working in a professional environment and the security of having a strong leader. Ask him about his behavior before granting him access to wonderful things like the loveseat or dinner.

Taking Control Of Your Dog's Life

What actions can you take to guarantee the success of your dog training? These are just a few actions you may want to consider to improve your dog's comprehension of you.

Taking charge of the pack

As you may know, dogs function according to a rank system or hierarchy. Dogs are considered to have a leader in this sense, known as the "alpha." Your dog would not follow your commands if you allowed him to have his way because he would think he was in charge. It's important to establish a distinct boundary between you and your dog.

Being in charge does not equate to being a bully. You must guide your dog in an advantageous manner to both of them. To ensure your dog understands that you are the boss, you may do a few things. Here are a few of them:

Find out whether your dog has problems with dominance.

Your dog may struggle with dominance and seek a leader to follow if he persistently barks at people in parks or bites his leash when you go on walks together. In this situation, you must assume the pack leader position to help your dog feel less anxious.

Adopt a dog's perspective.

You must put yourself in your dog's shoes to better comprehend him. Giving him sweets or petting him does not always translate into mutual understanding. There are moments when you can say what you want to say to your dog just by looking them in the eye. After all, eyes are like windows to the soul.

Set limits

Leaders of packs sleep somewhere distinct from their followers. Don't let this circumstance be an exception to that guideline. Couch or other areas that belong to you, take him out of those areas, and ensure he knows he has a place to sleep.

simple commanding

Give your dog some time to become acquainted with the simple commands you can give him. You may teach him maneuvers such as sitting, jumping, and other skills that will come in handy for you and your dog.

Going to the vet

The vet must acknowledge that he or she is your dog's pal. Your dog needs to know that his veterinarian is a friend. You must comprehend how he or she feels to maintain his or her composure. Imagine finding yourself in an unfamiliar environment, surrounded by people you don't know. If you were in that situation, what would you think? These are some strategies you may implement to help your dog remain composed during his first visit to the veterinarian.

With your dog, pretend to be a doctor.

Follow the same procedures a veterinarian would recommend if you brought your dog or puppy in for a routine examination. Examine your dog's mouth, open it, and check his ears, among other things. Acclimate him to the procedures that may be performed on him when your dog visits the veterinarian.

Visit the veterinarian frequently.

To ensure that your dog is not afraid when the time comes for him to visit the vet, it is important to acclimate him to coming in and out of the office. Take him there on a visitation basis or for routine checkups so he can become familiar with the staff and not fear them in the future.

Make veterinary days enjoyable.

Treat your dog to one of his or her favorite activities after the veterinarian visit. Afterward, perhaps allow him or her to play with him or her or go swimming. This is necessary so the dog will remember that visiting the veterinarian will result in exciting activities later on, making vet visits something to look forward to.

putting your dog to sleep outside

You may take steps to ensure your dog understands the rules in your house. You don't need to worry yourself or your dog out throughout this procedure, even though it could cause you some anxiety. Here are some points you should remember.

establishing a schedule

It's important to teach your dog a daily regimen that they can perform without fail. For instance, you may take him or her for a stroll every morning. As the weeks pass, the dog will start going for walks alone without a leash, and you will need to give him a treat or a condescending glance. This will facilitate the process of training your dog to comply with future house rules that you establish.

Mealtime routine

You must establish a feeding plan for your dog if you want them to learn more self-control. Feeding times must be established until your dog becomes accustomed to them. This is to prevent him or her from constantly requesting food. It also facilitates your housetraining.

Never punish your dogs for misbehavior.

You make mistakes because you're human, but dogs also do. Your dog doesn't need to be punished for his misdeeds. It takes commitment to care for your dog; part of that commitment is providing positive reinforcement. Simply remind him of the proper course of action when he commits something that cannot be undone.

Excavating

Dogs naturally dig, and when they do so, it's often assumed that they are being disobedient. In the wild, however, dogs would build lairs to defend themselves from predators and to raise their young. As a result, remember that your dog's digging in the yard is driven by instinct and natural necessity.

Although some dogs may turn this habit into an obsession, most seem to like it. Remembering that digging is safe for your dog and can be therapeutic and calming under proper supervision is also crucial.

This does not, however, imply that you won't suffer from your dog's digging habits, as they frequently wreck flowerbeds and gardens. Because of this, you must minimize your dog's digging while striking a balance between his drive to play and his quantity of extra energy.

The Reasons Why Dogs Love

We need to find out why your dog is digging before we can handle the digging issues. Digging is typically a sign of boredom and excessive activity in your dog, which results from inadequate stimulation.

Well-known breeds like Labrador and Retrievers frequently have excess energy and want a lot of exercise. It's critical to take these breeds for frequent walks, provide them with enough playtime, and prevent them from being left alone in the yard. If you let them be alone, they might quickly begin digging to release any extra energy. Keep in mind that, in contrast to us people, dogs cannot engage in hobbies like sports, watching television, or reading when they feel the need, so they turn to digging. Although this seems harmful to us, your dog enjoys it and uses it to eliminate extra energy.

An answer for digging

Instead of trying to change your dog's behavior, spend some time figuring out what you can do to minimize the cause of his digging. The first things you should think about are taking your dog for longer walks, playing with him in your yard, making sure he gets enough exercise, and making sure you are attending to all of his needs daily. Remember that your dog will become bored if you leave him alone in the backyard all day, and you can't expect to come home to a peaceful yard.

The next step is to identify the places you wish to keep digging out of and use fences or partitions to keep digging from happening there. Moreover, you can use materials like garden bed sheeting or boulders from your yard to hide the spots where your dog likes to dig. Since dogs don't want to dig through difficult places, you can more easily confine your dog and lessen their digging activity by adopting techniques like these. Finally, a less intrusive way to prevent your dog from digging in particular locations is to apply natural dog repellents like citronella, red pepper flakes, or pennyroyal oil.

The final phase is to rewire your dog's brain to eliminate ideas and preconceptions about undesirable behaviors, including digging. Training or obedience school is a simple solution, particularly with energetic dogs. This retrains your dog's thought process and behavior patterns. Your dog will focus on learning commands through training rather than digging. These substitutes taught directives that you can control positively for the requirement for undesirable or negative behavior.

To sum up, it's crucial to remember that if you leave your dog in the yard or garden, it's ideal to provide him with plenty of toys, bones, or other distractions like other dogs so he can burn off extra energy and you can save your garden in the process.

Recognize The Drives And Instincts Of The Dutch Shepherd

One exceptional breed that is well-known for its flexibility, intelligence, and agility is the Dutch Shepherd. Understanding this breed's urges and instincts is essential for training and socialization. This information will guarantee a contented and well-behaved Dutch Shepherd and assist you in successfully navigating the training process.

Senses:

1. Herding Instinct: Dutch Shepherds have a strong herding instinct because they are a breed that has a long history of working with farms and shepherds.

This implies that they might act like circling, biting at heels, or attempting to gather kids or other animals. Using suitable training and mental stimulation to channel and reroute this impulse is critical.

2. Protective Instinct: Dutch Shepherds want to protect their families and owners. They are great guard dogs because of their loyalty and protectiveness. However, this protective instinct can become excessively territorial or aggressive against outsiders if not properly trained and socialized. Early socialization is essential to ensure this protective instinct is in check and balance.

Motives:

1. Prey Drive: Because they were originally intended to be working farm dogs, Dutch Shepherds have a strong prey drive. Because of this urge, they chase and catch smaller creatures like squirrels, rabbits, and even small pets. It's crucial to provide them with mental and physical stimulation to control this drive. Playing games like fetch, hide-and-seek, or puzzle toys can help them appropriately and, in moderation, fulfill their prey drive.

2. Play Drive: Dutch Shepherds are eager to participate in games and interactive training sessions because of their high play drive. You and your dog can use this motivation to make training enjoyable and interesting. Positive reinforcement

of desired behaviors can be achieved by introducing interactive toys during training or using play as a reward for obedience.

One of your most fundamental duties as its guardian is to train your dog and ensure it is secure and fed.

You train your dog to suppress her animal impulses, prevent her from getting into situations where she could hurt you or other people, or just make her life happier and more meaningful.

Training is one of the best ways to develop a longer-lasting, more fulfilling relationship with your dog, especially when it involves a positive reinforcement-based approach.

Setting up the classroom

You must train your dog after you've decided to own one. You must think out what you will teach your dog. In addition to getting ready and your dog ready, you must create an environment conducive to learning.

The following advice can help you create a more dog-training-friendly environment in your home:

Go through this. The first step in the process is learning more about dogs, their behavior, and training techniques.

Make your house dog-proof.

Avoid frustrating and time-consuming situations if you discover, for example, that your dog has destroyed your house or trampled through your garden. Preventing these situations altogether is sometimes the best course of action.

Keep garbage and other items that dogs typically find appealing out of your dog's line of sight.

Give your dog a place to fully express its untainted primal impulses. If necessary, redecorate your house and set aside a room—like a baby nursery—either inside or outside your house just for your dog.

This can be the park if your home is cramped for space. Just be sure your dog knows that's the only place it can go around and jump up and down, and it's not inside your house.

This area might be as tiny as a living room nook where you keep your dog's toys. This is a useful suggestion if you don't want your dog to get used to biting on your leather couches.

CHAPTER 8: The Proper Way To Train Puppies With Clickers

A puppy clicker is a little, portable gadget that, when pressed, produces an auditory click. This tool is crucial for training little animals. This gadget is highly effective with puppies as it has remedies in the clicker.

Any puppy will begin clicker puppy training at a young age. Puppy clickers are popular among owners and trainers because of their ease of use and high success rate. You may find it helpful to study some of these tips if you intend to utilize a puppy-training clicker before beginning the training:

A fun technique to train a dog for many tasks is through clicker puppy training. Get your clicker ready and take care of all the preparation for your pocket. To ensure you and your dog have countless training sessions, purchase a dependable clicker.

Before you click puppy training bond with your dog, take him for a stroll. Then, following an exercise, resume your training. Before your puppy notices the sounds, press a few times. After ten clicks, reward yourself. Till the dog can identify the sound, keep repeating it.

Tell the dog to sit before you click once, as they will come to understand that the click signifies a treat. When you click on the behavior, give him a treat. When you press and treat giving continually, teach one action or trick. After some clicking and rewarding, your dog will eventually understand.

Once he's mastered one trick, teach him another and repeat the action. Always click and handle.

If your puppy picks up a lot of tricks from clicking, keep clicking without enjoying yourself.

To create more space for games, train your puppy outside. Once some preparation has been done, reassure and commend any beneficial conduct.

For novices and experts, the clicker is an invaluable tool for training animals worldwide. Not only do horses and puppies use the clicker method, but birds, mice, and even cats do as well. The dog's therapies are the sole drawback of clicker puppy training.

An overweight puppy might result from several therapies. Make careful to offer your dog fewer treats high in calories if you click and reward it every time. Treats can be substituted with pats and a chew toy because they follow the clicking procedure. If he gains a little weight, give him lots of labor to burn extra calories. Play games with your dog to get some exercise for both of you.

A dog may be an important possession in your house. Having a dog will greatly benefit your children. Regardless of technique, training must be cautious and consistent.

Reward good conduct and correct bad behavior frequently. Possess a dominant tone of voice. Never hit or break your dog for training since this can make the dog aggressive.

Between World Wars I and II

Dogs were considered pets until the First and Second World Wars when things became more difficult. Dogs were then called upon to carry out their primary responsibilities: serving humans. German shepherds and other breeds were trained to pull wagons and machine gun carriages and attack the opposing army. Dogs were also taught to find injured soldiers and retrieve medical assistance.

But because the First and Second World Wars were hard times, many armies employed canines instead of human soldiers. One such application was blasting tanks (caution: this is bad for dog lovers with soft hearts). After starving them, dogs would be lowered into tanks to be detonated. The dogs rarely survived, but happily, a very small number of them did.

Throughout conclusion, dogs were used as mascots throughout tumultuous times. In this sense, Smoky, a Yorkshire terrier found in New Guinea in 1944, is among the greatest instances. She bonded with her own Corporal William Wynne and went on 12 combat missions, 150 air raids, and a typhoon with him. She even prevented him from dying by warning him about a burst of gunfire that had killed eight other troops who were nearby. But Smoky's primary objective was to amuse soldiers, whether performing their duties or recuperating in various hospitals around the globe.

Dogs' Current Role and Purpose

Dogs of today can perform several tasks at once. When taught to identify persons buried under rubble or detect drugs and bombs, they not only protect their owners but also save lives. They also support athletes who hunt, race, or help the disabled live somewhat independently. Furthermore, dogs still serve as status symbols for their owners, so fashionistas show off their little, jeweled, and robed Chihuahuas while rough dudes own pit bulls.

Dogs have always served the same purposes but also fulfill a purpose unique to the modern era: companionship. Having a pet used to be considered a luxury, but these days, it's more of a need, particularly for people who experience loneliness or get lonely after losing or moving on from loved ones. Because of their unselfish and unconditional devotion, dogs have been shown to melt people's hearts; for this reason, even psychiatrists recommend them to persons who are depressed.

You must acknowledge that your dog is truly someone worth talking to after going through this entire journey through their past. If so, you're finally prepared to discover how your four-legged companion has attempted to communicate with you via the Dog Language.

Remain. Obedience to your dog requires that you teach him to stay. Your dog may occasionally be tempted to misbehave or face danger, in which case you may be able to command him to "stay" to keep things under control.

It's crucial to avoid forcing your dog to "stay" somewhere for an extended period unless there is a compelling reason to do so. It is fine to have your dog "stay" longer when you are hosting a guest with a small child and are worried that your dog might jump on the child. However, don't make him "sit" for an extended period just to "sit."

To attain this objective, your dog will require a leash and a collar that fits snugly but comfortably.

● Make your dog sit. Give him something for doing it. Then, tell him to "stay" while you extend your hand in a "halt" gesture, facing him with the palm and interior of your hand facing him.

● Reward your dog if he obeys, even if it was an accident.

● Then, as you face him and back away, repeat the order to "stay." Give him a prize if he does. You could want to say his name along with the "Stay" prompt, like "Joe, stay." You have the last say on it.

● Go over the lesson again, but put greater space between you and your dog as you back away. Then, move to a place where he can't see you to escalate the situation. Give him something to eat when he stays put.

● Once he has "Stayed" for as long as you want him to, give him the cue "Up" to continue moving. Some people like "Okay," but I choose "Up" because it sounds so much like "Stay". Whichever verbal cue you decide on, be consistent with it, let him know that it indicates he can move, and give him a reward when he does.

Come on over here. Instructing your dog to come when called will go a long way toward keeping him safe and out of trouble. No matter the circumstances, an obedient dog is expected to come when called.

● Tell your dog to "Come" when he is engaged in an activity. Hold a reward in one hand and make it seem attractive to do so. Give him a treat and some praise when he comes to you and reacts.

● Use a long leash and gently tug on your dog to urge him to come to you if he is not complying.

● Continue increasing the task's difficulty and cue him to "Come" when he is doing something he enjoys, eating, or even falling asleep. The distance he must travel to reach you gets progressively greater.

● When your dog obeys, express your appreciation for his good conduct and give him something in return.

Stop. Your dog may learn this lesson more than all others. When your dog is chasing a car or a child, it might not be suitable to tell him to "Sit" or "Lay Down," but the command "Halt" is okay in this circumstance and is the one that is most frequently used to stop many problematic behaviors that entail such harmful behavioral concerns.

● Give your dog the verbal indication to "Halt" when you abruptly cease playing or walking him. Stop all movements, and give him a reward when he follows suit.

● Increase the intensity of this exercise when he is engaged in any intense physical activity that he enjoys, such as chasing a ball. Thank him for following your instructions.

● When your dog starts a malicious quest, like chasing a cat or chasing a herd of cows, use this trigger. It is best to schedule it in advance to prepare you to interrupt if he doesn't.

Pursuing. Your dog may acquire the dangerous negative behavior of chasing naturally or by volition. Dogs have a natural "flight or fight" response, and because they are dogs, they tend to chase. However, the actions should not be accepted. It poses a serious risk to you, your dog, and other people and animals.

● Before you chase, pay attention to your dog's cues. While some dogs suddenly take off, others focus on the target or give warning signs beforehand. Stop him from pursuing by diverting his attention before he gives up on the chase and praising him for stopping.

● Give your dog the order to "Halt" if he does run after something. If he ignores your cue, it's time to repeat his formal instruction on the "Halt" order.

Educing Your Spanish

Remember that the puppy is nearly as capable of understanding our signs as a baby, so don't give up on teaching them your language. It's important to keep a few things in mind when you're ready to teach your puppy what a word entails and that you want to see something specific done when the word is spoken. For example, "down" (as in "lie down") should only be used once; do not say "Down, down, down, down." When a word is used repeatedly, there are two problems: Initially, your dog might mistake the word you speak for "Downdowndowndown." Second, your dog might decide to consistently wait until you reach the fourth repetition of "down" if she eventually discovers the phrase's meaning and realizes that you are just saying it four times.

Though there are certain exceptions, in certain situations, you might say something like "Down" and then repeat it once more for emphasis if you want your puppy to stay in that position for more than a few seconds ("Yes, down!"). That is not the same as speaking the term you teach several times. You should be concise and unambiguous. Simply respond "No," and then retain the reward if your puppy does not perform the action you have demonstrated. You may have to quit training.

When educating them for the first time, giving a word to a puppy after they act is essential. Therefore, when it comes to "Down," use hand signals and a lure to encourage your puppy to go into a down position; after they've laid down, reward them with a treat and say, "Down!" once at a normal volume—there's no need to yell.

Comprehending THE CUES OF YOUR DOG

Teaching our dogs to understand us is vital, but we must also learn how they communicate back. Anyone who has ever shared a home with a puppy understands that relationships are two-way streets, and their many displays of barking, growling, and whining have meaning. Thanks to their incredibly expressive body language, you can distinguish between your puppy's hungry bark, an enthusiastic, playful bark, and a bark directed at a stranger. In addition, puppies communicate nonverbally to convey their emotions, just like people. You can tell the difference between a snarl that says, "Let's play!" and one that says, "Step back," by observing certain puppy attitudes and motions.

The meaning of your pet's nonverbal cues will vary depending on the circumstances and the particular puppy.

In light of how crucial it is to understand your puppy's cues and the circumstances around them, the following are some general things to look out for:

- Tail: A standing tail usually indicates interest; when combined with other non-verbal cues that indicate happiness, a swaying tail suggests that the puppy is happy or eager to play. The puppy may swing purposefully and moderately if unsure of something, but a tucked tail suggests fear and anxiety.

- Ears: When a puppy's ears are drawn back, they may be afraid or nervous because they listen to what is happening behind them. The puppy is probably interested in something or has heard something when it prickles forward.

- Eyes: As you get to know your puppy more, you can quickly read their thoughts and mood by observing their eyes. They are terrified of something nearby if their pupils dilate, dart from side to side, or show the whites of their eyes. A quick, serious look could indicate danger or a strong desire to play with you.

• Mouth: Puppies often close their jaws, show teeth, and twitch their lips when afraid. A fidgety puppy may frequently lick its lips and pant. Nevertheless, a puppy with its tongue out and mouth open may be happy or content; if it is panting, it may be uncomfortable or warm.

• Posture: While timid or fearful puppies typically hunch to the ground, confident puppies stand tall. A relaxed puppy indicates that they are at ease in that environment.

Avoid Leaping

Dogs welcome their loved ones by jumping on them, especially you, his alpha master and the source of everything. They would like to be touched, are delighted to see you again, and want to express their affection for you. Their method of saying, "Look at me!" is to jump. In a little dog or puppy, this could be adorable, but as the dog reaches thirty pounds or more, it might cause problems. In addition to potentially upsetting and uncomfortable guests, it can negatively rather than positively affect your family's get-togethers when your dog is well-behaved. Large breeds can scratch your legs, soil your dress or pants, throw you off balance while greeting you on your hind legs, or cause you to trip and fall when you go through the door with your groceries. It takes place. Consequently, begin teaching your dog—regardless of size—that it is not appropriate to jump on people.

Say "Whoa" to begin with when your dog jumps on you. After that, exit the room. A few seconds later, reenter and repeat as needed. When he climbs on you, it won't sit well with him if you go.

Naturally, you can also advise him to stop jumping on other people, and you can even ask your family and friends to assist you in training him by having them give him the "Whoa" sound and exit the room.

Give your French Bulldog lots of cuddles and affection when he stops jumping on you. To pet him, stoop to his level. When you're ready, you'll give him attention at his level, so you don't need to jump on him to get it.

You can utilize the time-out approach if your French Bulldog will not stop leaping on people despite your best efforts to train him or if he exhibits other attention-seeking behaviors, such as awkward leg humping. When he jumps, humps, or does anything else you find objectionable, just take him out of the room and tie him up for a short while. Naturally, only use this as a last resort. When he is finally well-trained, he will immediately obey your commands, and you will become the dominant dog.

Not biting

All dogs naturally display the behavior of chewing. That's why he offers you that amazing Hollywood smile with 42 long, pointed teeth. Chewing aids in your dog's dental health. Teething puppies are particularly likely to chew on anything that fits into their mouths.

Giving your French Bulldog chew toys and safe, healthy bones will keep his mouth active and his mind somewhat engaged when bored.

If your dog is chewing on something, like your new shoe, take it out immediately and give him the cold shoulder. Change it out for a bone or a toy. Say, "Well done, boy."

You can apply a deterrent spray, such as Granniks-Bitter-Apple or citronella, to make something undesirable to him if he doesn't leave it alone. If it tastes bad, he won't want to chew on it.

Not Excavating

Many dogs are fond of digging. This is what certain dogs, like Frenchies, do since digging for food is in their genetic makeup. Some breeds do this to make a cool burrow where they may lie down and cool off, such as huskies and malamutes. Some, however, just do it for fun. Dogs are uniquely attracted to soft mud and sand, which can be challenging to overcome.

You should train your French Bulldog to dig only in designated areas to prevent digging. If feasible, provide him with a designated digging area where you won't object if he excavates. Let him dig for toys or bones you've buried in the ground. The majority of canines adore this exercise.

Tell your French Bulldog dog "No" as you bury the location in front of him when he digs in other areas that are not acceptable. Additionally, you can stuff coins, bottle caps, and other garbage into a can. Watch your dog and stay hidden. Hit that can, shocking him the moment he starts to dig. He won't be as tempted to dig once he starts associating digging with the unpleasant sound of the shaking can.

Not a Barking

Prevention is the key to teaching your dog not to bark. The minute something happens, he is excited to see you or feels scared or interested by a far-off noise or knock at the door; you want to educate him not to bark his adorable, furry little head off. Teach him to divert his attention and occupy himself with one of the other activities we covered above when he is bored or frustrated rather than just standing there barking at nothing and upsetting you and your neighbors.

As you are well aware, dogs naturally bark. It is his reaction to many different things. He can be warning you of impending danger when he barks. He might be telling dogs or other animals to keep away. He might bark to let you know where he's claimed territory or to let you know he's excited to play. Alternatively, he might be bored and enjoy barking to kill time. My dog says that if I sleep too long, he will bark at me to wake me up. When they feel like it, dogs use what they have cleverly. I let it happen because it's not often that this happens, but I find it amusing that he thought to yell at me to wake up.

Due to their intelligence, energy, and desire to please other dogs, Wirehaired Pointing Griffons are amenable to positive reinforcement training methods. The following are some effective training methods for wirehaired pointers:

1. Treat-Based Training: Use little, delicious goodies as a means of rewarding desired actions. Reward your Griffon when they obey a demand, like sitting or staying. This favorable association upholds the conduct that requires energizing.

2. Clicker Training: Use a clicker, a little device that produces a distinct clicking sound, as a reward for appropriate conduct. Match the snap with a treat to

show your Griffon that they've ever figured things out. They can better grasp when they have completed the perfect exercise with the help of this strategy.

3. Consistency and Patience: Adhere to directives and presumptions consistently. Rely on comparable cues for specific tasks, and exercise patience while your Griffon picks up new skills. Reinforcement and repetition help to solidify their comprehension.

4. Verbal Praise and Fondness: Accompany treats with loving gestures such as caressing or belly rubs. Positive reinforcement involves more than simply food; Wirehaired Pointing Griffons respond enthusiastically to displays of affection and approval.

5. Quick, Intense Training Sessions: Keep training sessions brief to prevent your Griffon from becoming weary or overworked (10–15 minutes). To keep the meetings interesting, encourage participation and give them frequent praise for their efforts.

6. Avoid Discipline: Give up using harsh punishment or chastisement. These methods may cause your Griffon to become nervous or disorganized, hindering their growth. Positive reinforcement is more about empowering appropriate behavior than rejecting bad behavior.

7. Trustworthy Daily Routine: Establish a daily routine for feeding, walks, and training sessions. Schedules benefit

Wirehaired Pointing Griffons since they help them better comprehend expectations and behavior.

Step 6 in Chapter 7

Congratulations on completing Step 6 of the housetraining procedure! This chapter explains how to transition your dog from supervised to unsupervised time so that, over time, they can grow into confident, well-mannered friends.

Transitioning From Watched To Unwatched Time

When your dog becomes more proficient at housebreaking, you can gradually increase their freedom and independence. Gradually expand your dog's access area within your house at first, but always keep a watch on them. This deliberate approach maintains a secure learning environment and prevents your pet from becoming overstimulated.

Throughout this change, observe how your dog behaves. Consider temporarily lowering the level of independence and providing more guidance and reinforcement for positive behavior if errors occur.

Getting Your Dog to Believe in Himself

Increasing your dog's sense of self-worth is crucial for their overall well-being and helping them successfully housebreak. Use strategies for positive reinforcement to encourage positive behavior in your kids even as you offer them more freedom. Recognize achievements and provide a secure, caring home for your dog to enable them to develop and prosper.

Gradually introduce your dog to new situations, people, and events by giving them new experiences. This deliberate approach gives them confidence and makes it easier to adjust to different situations without feeling overwhelmed.

Remember that each dog grows at a unique pace. For some people, more freedom may be acceptable sooner rather than later. Observe the cues your dog offers you and adjust your strategy accordingly. The goal is to assist your pet in gaining a sense of independence and responsibility while building a solid bond based on trust and positive reinforcement.

By the time this chapter finishes, you'll know exactly how to handle the transition from supervised to unsupervised time, ensuring that you and your dog will always be a self-assured, well-mannered team. Come celebrate your successful housetraining achievements with us at the last step, 7:

Celebrate Success. Here, we'll offer encouragement for good behavior to guarantee long-term outcomes.

How to stop your dog from barking nonstop

Canines emit barks. That cannot be avoided in any manner. However, you can stop them from barking. Some individuals will even go so far as to pay for surgery or use shock collars on their dogs, but those are horrible methods to take.

Inside your home with a straightforward technique. Make use of a spray bottle.

At this stage, you'll need to exercise caution and give him a quick spritz every time he barks inside your home. This won't harm your pet; it will simply surprise him enough to change his mood. If you spray him enough, he'll learn he cannot bark inside the house.

You can also employ this tactic if he does anything that bothers you. Biting on shoes and other furnishings is one example. A gentle mist from the water should make him retreat quickly to his crate's safety and reflect on his current choices.

Dogs react to rewards the best.

Praise your puppy appropriately whenever he performs a good deed if you want him to be well-mannered and obedient. Give him praise or incentives if he follows instructions on time. Your dog should experience ecstasy after a nice stroking session, and he should essentially smile for the remainder of the day.

The best method is positive reinforcement; never strike your puppy, as this will not help.

Finally, but just as importantly, always reward them on schedule.

Chapter 6: Having Fun with Your Puppy

After hearing all this, you would believe owning a puppy is all labor and no fun. Every day you spend with your puppy will contribute to a long and healthy relationship between you and him.

If you train him, your dog will have something to do and look forward to when he is with you. In addition, he will know when and how to behave appropriately in your company or the presence of others.

Give your puppy time to learn how to behave; don't expect it to do so immediately. It takes a lot of time to train a dog properly. This is not a task that can be completed in a single day. It will take a few days or perhaps weeks for them to comprehend what is anticipated of them. Remain calm; after all, they are incapable of comprehending human language. But they will eventually understand your behaviorand the rewards system you set up, so be upbeat and enjoy training your puppy.

All appreciate a well-behaved dog, and as a result, he will receive all the love and care required to get through the day from everyone.

Make sure you spend time playing with your pet following each training session. He can be readily trained to chase a ball around your backyard for exercise, or you can teach him to play fetch.

After each training and play session, make sure you both unwind. There's nothing quite like having a contented dog when you unwind.

Myth: A puppy cannot begin training until six months old.

Reality: The "old fashioned" teaching techniques that used actual collar adjustments are the source of this misconception. Consequently, a dog was preferred to be at least old enough to don the collar, bear the burden of neckline attachments, and maintain discipline during the training sessions. There's no reason you couldn't start working with your dog as soon as possible, especially with the best dog training programs available today that provide positive reinforcement and opportunities for interaction with your pet.

When dogs can see and recognize things in their environment, they learn the lessons. A puppy's attention span may be less than an adult dog's. Therefore, training may need to be more persistent. Still, there's no reason why your puppy can't start adopting right away, and the earlier you start, the quicker your puppy will pick up the skills.

For your puppy to develop into a well-mannered and mature dog, you must introduce him to new people and objects as soon as possible.

Myth: "Uplifting feedback or positive reinforcement" training only works with small, happy dogs; it does not work with very strong, obstinate, or fierce canines.

Reality: Trainers of interesting warm-blooded land and marine species typically employ uplifting feedback as a basic training technique. If you can focus on rewarding behaviors to train a large predator, like a tiger or killer whale, there's no reason you can't do the same with your dog, regardless of his breed. Furthermore, as the study strengthens our understanding of behavior, it is generally agreed upon that using unpleasant training methods on fearsome or uncooperative canines is more likely to produce terrible outcomes. However, if we focus on making up for the dog's discomfort and easing its worries, we'll see calmer dogs and more grounded human-animal relationships.

Myth: Because he is dominant, my dog does pull his chain; because he is dominating, my dog hops on me; because he is overwhelming, my puppy lies on the lounge chair; or because he is dominating, my dog won't let me even touch his nail.

Reality: Almost all inappropriate behavior in dogs that causes owners to lose their cool has been explained away by the concept of "predominance." The problem lies in the phrase "dominance," which is completely incorrect when used by most dog caretakers and, regrettably, some coaches today. A social relationship between two or more persons is depicted by predominance. It's not a quality of a character. Unlike what many believe, canines don't spend their energy attempting to gain control over people.

If your dog jumps on you, it's probably because he hasn't learned that this isn't a good habit. If he tugs at his leash, he has not been trained to walk as close to you as possible. The clippers and brush are likely uncomfortable, frightening, or both if he doesn't care to be groomed. The moral of the story is to choose what you need your dog to do, continue demonstrating that to him, and reward him for doing it correctly. If your dog is doing something you don't care about, don't worry about "dominance."

Myth: Feeding a dog during training equates to enticing it.

Reality: Although feeding a dog can "influence" it, the statement above demonstrates a severe lack of understanding of the laws of learning hypothesis. When you display a creature, any creature, including human beings! Something fresh, a reward (or, more precisely, a "fortification") for "hitting the nail on the head," and an indication that you succeeded should be included.

For individuals, this could be a reward or salary from your job or an A+ from a teacher. All animals "work" for defenses, and dogs are no different. Although most dogs love food and believe it is worth working for, mentors frequently use it as compensation. However, we can also use toys, play, work, stroking, cheerful conversation, and other activities. A reward or fortification is shown to a creature to demonstrate that they are correct. A creature can be motivated to perform a task they are capable of by being given an influence.

Myth: Wearing a head collar might hurt your neck and spine.

Reality: wearing head collars and suffering injuries to their necks or spines. When used properly, these collars shouldn't have any adverse physical effects on your dog.

Myth: I've heard my dog should work for me just to make me happy.

Reality: Since it satisfies their expectations, dogs finally act in the ways that they do. Having animals that seem to value our conversations and to be a part of our lives is a blessing for us as humans. However, we must recognize that this is a partnership and that dogs benefit from our relationships in several ways, including receiving affection, play, shelter, and sustenance.

In this sense, we shouldn't assume that a dog "just needs to satisfy us" when it accomplishes something that makes us happy. They are trying to cheer us up because it also earns them a reward, a belly rub, or other fantastic circumstances. Suppose you believe in the psychological hypothesis that a dog should only do things to please you and never receive reinforcement or rewards for meeting your needs. In that case, you will probably end up with a difficult-to-train dog because he struggles to recognize when he has done something correctly without your reinforcement.

Myth: An older dog won't cling to you, learn new tricks, or get along with other families. This is because "an old puppy can't learn new traps."

Reality: A dog, or any other species, may be trained at any age. However, remember that an animal's experience level may indicate how much they have ingrained behavior that you now need to adjust. It might take a little longer to alter that behavior in light of this. However, there are a few instances where training an experienced dog can be less difficult than training a puppy. More mature dogs tend to be more attentive and thoughtful when working with you since they are generally more settled than young puppies.

Developing into a Pack Leader at Home

Dog training can be accomplished using various techniques, all of which have advantages. The best results are frequently obtained by combining several techniques, but your mutt must regard you as the pack leader. Mother Nature has established this as a rule; it is not voluntary.

Dogs are pack animals that will always look for a leader. You must renounce normal democratic behavior and establish a dictatorship in which you will serve as the designated leader. Your pet will try to assume the role of leader if he doesn't perceive you as one, which frequently results in aggressive and/or destructive behavior.

Making yourself known as the Alpha in the house is crucial, regardless of whether you have an older dog you adopted or a brand-new puppy. When done correctly, this may be an enjoyable exercise that will make your dog's environment healthier rather than stressful.

Adhering to these few straightforward guidelines can establish yourself as the Alpha and relieve your dog of tension. Your home will feel more serene, and the benefits of having a pet, regardless of age or breed, will soon become evident.

First rule: Be the owner of your house.

Your dog must understand his limits from an early age. As the pack leader, you can restrict access to certain locations, such as furniture. You have to let your dog inside of his designated zones when you first embark on your journey to become the pack leader. Ensure your dog has access to cozy floor beds and cushions, but don't let him use the furniture! When Fido politely asks for access to the furniture, you can grant it after you're confident he knows who is in charge.

Second rule: Manage the food

Distribution of food is another sign of leadership. The pack leader will always eat first in the wild, and the other pack members must adhere to a pecking order. People must perceive you and your family as more important than your pet. When the family is having supper, your dog should ideally sleep peacefully in a different room and not participate in any activities.

You should establish your control over your dog's survival from an early age. Your dog should be able to refuse food and drink from you without showing any signs of aggression. You will have proven that you are your pack's leader and have complete control over your pet's survival after he learns that you provide for all his necessities. Your pet must behave properly around food, and you can prevent aggressive behavior—which frequently results in issues during mealtimes—by practicing self-control.

Rule#3: Come and go whenever you like

Many pet owners struggle with separation anxiety, a well-known issue that makes their nervous animals unable to be left alone for extended periods. All this conduct tells you is that your dog doesn't think you can handle life away from home! Your dog will worry that he is not with you to protect you and make sure you return home safely if you cannot demonstrate your strength as a leader.

A healthy pack confidently awaits the leader's return and waits patiently for him to do so. Your home should experience the same thing. Your dog won't be anxious when you leave and will wait patiently for you to return if he trusts your leadership skills. It should also be a low-key event to leave the house. Just bid them farewell and go out without a fuss. When you return, the same kind of easygoing greetings from both of you should apply. We all know how much joy it can bring to come home to a joyful, excited dog, but to help resolve anxiety-related problems, it's best to handle repeat visits more casually and slow down the process.

I hope that this book has been very beneficial to you thus far. I sincerely hope that you are!

Could you please assist me? I want to give this book to as many aspiring dog owners as possible to give them something worthwhile to read that doesn't take too long. I would be very grateful if you could write a brief, candid, and open review. That would be excellent!

Bringing Your Dachshund Home

Getting Ready for the Initial Day

Preparation is essential to ensure a seamless first day at home with your dachshund. To prepare, adhere to these rules:

Provides

Ensure everything you need—food, bowls, collars, leashes, crates, potty pads, cleaning supplies, and toys—is pre-purchased and set up. Potty accidents will inevitably occur during the first week, so stock up on puppy pads, pet stain remover, and paper towels.

Verify the House

Ensure your house is safe again, and remove any puppy-level hazards. Use gates to bar your dachshund from entering any areas or rooms that you don't want him to explore. Completely proof the space or room your pet will first be inside.

Selecting a Space

Choose a single room, such as the living room, bedroom, or kitchen, and introduce your dachshund there first. An excess of space could be intimidating. This room needs to be completely secured with no valuables or potential dangers. Arrange the kennel such that food, water, bedding, and newspaper are all close at hand.

Introduction to Crates

Empty the open crate of food to create a positive association. Your dachshund will feel more at ease entering the crate if you start feeding them in it from day one. Build up to quick five- to ten-minute closed-door sessions after beginning cautiously with shorter trial periods during which the door is left open.

Rest Area

Choose a spot for your outdoor toilet that is near your outer door. To confirm this is the proper place to relieve yourself, take your dog there often. Keep a careful eye on things, and don't immediately give them free rein in the yard. For the initial training, think about using disposable toilet pads.

Sensitization to Sound

Dachshunds may have hearing issues. Turn down the volume on your TV, music, and vacuum cleaner soundtracks to help your dog become used to everyday noises in the house. Wean kids off of the noises they will hear daily.

Hold Off Until Ready

When you have a few days to spare, pick up your dachshund to aid in their adjustment. Before a busy trip weekend or business obligations, don't bring them home right away. During the first two weeks, be prepared to devote time.

Timetable for the First Day

Be at home for bonding, supervision, and bathroom breaks. Maintain a consistent schedule for feeding, playing, napping, and training. Your dachshund will become used to their new surroundings and family members with frequent praise and rewards. Don't overdo the early introductions and stimulation.

Be Patient and Prepare

That first week, not everything will go as planned! You'll handle the early hurdles of bringing your pup home with care and understanding if you prepare for pee accidents, possible anxiety/crying, and setting up a safe, confined location for your dog.

Section Two

Fundamentals of Dog Training for Novices

A well-groomed dog is a pleasure to own, and training your dog sets the bar for compliance. Therefore, it is essential that the planning not be harsh. As it strengthens the attachment you are trying to form with your dog, the preparation should improve the relationship between you and your dog. If your dog is well-prepared, you can rely on him to respond to your commands promptly and consistently.

You will learn how to communicate with one another using a unique kind of language during the preparation. A lot of training is required for preparation, and consistent, meticulous discipline yields encouraging outcomes. The more time and effort you invest in training your dog, the greater the benefits you will reap. You may find many of them online if you require a professional mentor to help you train your new puppy. Whatever the case, the person who started the preparation gets ingrained with a dog's devotion. You could also consider enrolling in a preparatory course.

Your dog will learn the fundamental commands in the lesson, such as sit, stay, down, and come. He will also learn how to walk nicely while wearing a leash.

As part of training your dog, you should reward him with a small piece of a treat. Still, learning to communicate with the dog and understand his language is a good preparation step. This includes anticipating his responses and providing justification for anything from awarding prizes to making amends to inspire compliance.

How to Begin Training for Obedience

Start getting ready for a dog as soon as you get him back. You can begin demonstrating a few habits to him. Due to their limited attention span, dogs should only spend ten to fifteen minutes preparing for each meeting. This can be repeated several times regularly until your dog becomes proficient at it.

When getting ready, have a bag of candy close at hand. Give your small dog a treat every time he puts forth a lot of effort. Pay, though, is subject to change. You may pet him, provide him with a toy, or use spoken acknowledgment. After this, make commendatory movements like "Great kid! This will awaken and instill in him the importance of following your instructions.

Refrain from rewarding him with goodies in the middle of teaching sessions. If he receives gifts without earning them, he won't exert much effort in getting ready. Don't lose your cool and start yelling at your dog if he refuses to follow you. Just hold onto your prize.

This will convey to him that he must obey to obtain it.

Just One Word Will Do

Saying your sign just once is enough. Remember that a dog's hearing is keen, and he can always hear you the first time when they are really good. Repeating the prompt word several times will cause him to block you out like youth do.

Plan your workouts before meals.

Given that they are hungry, dogs are more considerate of their commands. They understand that they will receive a respectable portion of the delicious prize by complying.

Avoid Being Sidetracked During Your Training

You want to offer your dog every opportunity when you're getting ready. Avoid distractions by turning off your PDA and ignoring doorbells. For the first few sessions, you can have them in a large enough empty area to accommodate your dog's growth. When your dog can obey a few basic commands, you can take him outdoors into a gated area. If he is left unattended, always have a leash on him.

Make sure your dog has a comfortable environment for the training sessions. Don't yell at your small dog, no matter how irritated you are with him. When you shout at them, dogs will naturally become wary and distracted and stop paying attention to you.

Basic Instruction in Dog Obedience

These are some basic commands you can use to get your puppy ready.

How to Take a Seat

The "sit" order is the most fundamental of the comparatively large number of rudiments. Supervising your small dog once he learns to obey this command until he gains greater self-control will be easier.

Assume a level with your puppy and place a reward near his nose.

Raise your hand as his head follows the treat. His butt will land on the ground when his head follows your hand's movement. As soon as he succeeds in sitting on his butt, reward him with a treat and tell him how well he did. Until he masters the act, repeat this instruction as many times as needed.

Treats should never be held too high since your puppy will jump for them. Keep your hand closed and up so that he can't reach out with his neck to grab it. Say, "Good sit!" each time his butt reaches the ground."

Chapter 2: Teaching Your Dog to Eat

Frequently, positive remarks like "Excellent puppy!" and "Well done, dog! Even a quick slap on the back can be enough positive reinforcement for appropriate behavior. Sometimes, though, these strategies might not be effective. Dog treats are your best buddy in these trying times. Although this may make you laugh, treats are a crucial part of the dog training process.

Most puppies like sweets, and they will frequently do all it takes to obtain them. It is crucial to remember threats' power and employ them as leverage in trying circumstances. It's crucial to remember not to abuse this concept of rewards, though. When all else fails, break out the sweets! Treat your dog only when they genuinely deserve it.

Here are a few excellent methods you can apply to the food during the training process:

Your dog will undoubtedly try to jump up to get at the treat if you hold it in your hand just out of reach. After they accomplish this, instruct them to follow your "sit" order and reward them with the goodie.

Keep the treat out of your dog's reach by holding it in your hand. Give your dog the instruction to "stand." Incorporate this by shifting the food slightly in your palm so your dog can get up to smell it. It is recommended that you offer them the reward at this stage.

Your dog needs to practice these command-treat activities repeatedly to develop discipline; with the right training, your dog will be able to obey your directions right away. Pats and encouragement should always accompany food treats, as this will help reinforce the behavior positively.

Food Categories

Foods intended for training should be small, easily digested, and ideally free of crumbs (not because it makes cleanupeasier; it's merely a convenience). Bite-sized chunks of meat will work just fine; your neighborhood grocery shop has dog treats.

Small bits of string cheese or cheddar cheese are perfect for this type of training on dogs who are not lactose intolerant.

Typically, using bones is a bad idea since the dogs will become bored with the training and will only play with the bone for a long time.

You (and your dog, to some extent) have complete control over what they eat, but to properly condition your puppy, don't forget to include food rewards in their diet. In addition, do not forget to always give your dog vocal praise and attention in addition to food rewards since they desire the attention as much, if not more, than the treat itself.

Weaning Off of Reward Foods

Food rewards are a fantastic place to start when training your dog, but you should also consider weaning them off as soon as possible. As your dog improves in training and starts to comprehend your voice commands and tone of voice regarding specific behaviors, you can gradually wean him off.

A crucial phase in the training process is weaning your dog off treats as positive reinforcement so they don't become addicted to them and won't obey your directions unless food is available as a reward. This should not be too tough of a procedure because dogs, inherently friendly animals, get even more attracted to their owner's praise than the food they give them anyway.

The following is a quick rundown of several different treats that your dog will adore:

Playing quick games like tug-of-war, fetch, and catch

Following bubbles

Frisbee throwing

following a light beam, such as a flashlight

Use your dog's preference for one of these substitute treats to your advantage.

Bribe vs. Prize

You can't train your dog incorrectly if you don't know the difference between a bribe and a reward. Allow me to clarify. Let's say you teach your dog a new skill. When they master it, you give them a treat as a type of reward or positive reinforcement.

Do not treat your dog to coax obedience when you see that they are not following a command they have completed several times. This is known as bribery in the dog training community, so avoid doing it! Bribes only teach the dog that they don't have to do anything unless paid beforehand. Hence, a competent trainer will refrain from using them. Word to the wise: stay away from this in all facets of your life, not just when training dogs!

Weaning your dog off food treats as soon as possible is the greatest way to ensure that rewards don't become bribes. Start substituting "life rewards" for food rewards, such as going on a walk with your dog (they will adore this), getting them a toy to play with, or just cuddling up on the couch with them (this reward will probably be their favorite as they get older). Your dog will quickly learn that doors carrying different incentives will open for him or her if they obey your directions and pays attention to you; this will guarantee that the training process stays on course.

Toilet Training

We're going to talk about potty training next. The problem is that potty training and crate training go hand in hand. Your dog will instinctively go to his allotted bathroom location once you have put him inside his box.

As you are the one designating your dog's territory, you are the one in charge when you do this. For this reason, you might leave a section of your yard unfinished. Alternatively, you might designate a specific area within your home, like a pee pad.

Upon mastering the rhythm, he can navigate the crate, whether for resting or because you have imprisoned him for personal gain.

Here's another thing to keep in mind: take your German Shepherd to the restroom area you've set up for him around 10 minutes after feeding and watering him.

Given the high level of intelligence associated with German Shepherd breeds, it should not take long for your puppy to become accustomed to the schedule. Your dog will eventually be able to independently adhere to the schedule.

Your dog will begin to communicate with you when he wants to use the restroom, indicating that he has already grasped the concept of the entire procedure. Typically, when they need to urinate, they accomplish this by scratching at your door.

Your puppy has already finished toilet training if they have been doing that on a regular basis.

Teaching Yourself To Sit

Teaching your German Shepherd to sit is one of the first commands, if not the first. Now, there are numerous advantages associated with this command in particular. You can also use this to calm a hyperactive dog down before feeding them.

Of course, there are other circumstances in which this will be necessary for your convenience. Here's how to teach your puppy to sit as effectively as possible.

Take a handful of your dog's treats and conceal them with one hand.

To ensure your dog doesn't get distracted during training, locate a peaceful place in your home with few or no distractions.

Place your dog in front of you and stand up straight, ensuring you face the same direction.

Take a treat and hold it in your palm so that you may give your dog a hand signal with it. Don't give it to your dog just yet; he should be able to sniff it from your hand. This is only a ploy to get your dog's attention.

Hold the treat between your fingertips so your dog can see it once he has smelled it. Make sure the object is held slightly above your dog's nose. Maintain a high standard.

While holding your treat, push your arm forward and give the verbal order "sit." Your dog must stare at the treat, which is why you must do this. Because of the steep slope, he would be sitting.

Give your dog the treat in your palm as a reward when he sits. You can also express your love for him by giving him praise in words and with pets.

It can take your dog a few days to become used to this before he masters it completely. There will be instances in which he obeys the order and others in which he does not.

Simply keep doing this until he understands the command and can execute it without making mistakes. For this training session, it would be preferable to use smaller goodies, while larger treats could be broken up into smaller pieces.

If not, there's a chance that your dog could develop stomach issues or become overweight. You can gradually substitute other compliments and pets for food with practice and patience in this training.

Part Iv Of The Four C's 1

Although this may sound strange, four Cs are fundamental to training a submissive, well-mannered dog. These are focus, communication, consistency, and serenity. Most of us aspire to train our dogs or work as professional trainers, but this is a serious endeavor. You need to possess exceptional skills to become a trainer; it is not enough to just love dogs and wish to train them. If you love dogs, you become a dog trainer, not a dog owner.

The first two abilities of a competent trainer—one whose guidance can transform a puppy or dog into an obedient and well-behaved one—will be the subject of this chapter.

serenity

The most crucial quality a trainer needs to possess to discipline a recalcitrant student—in this case, a pack of dogs—is calmness. Calmness is the secret to every training session's success, whether it involves humans or animals. Dogs, like people, get accustomed to their mother's loving, kind, and soothing touch. They come to demand the same composure from their pack leader as they age. Dogs learn via observation; they do not come into the world knowing everything. As a dog trainer, you must exhibit the same composure if you want the dog to act sensibly and be calm.

If you, as a trainer, lose your cool and act impolitely, the dogs will probably follow suit. They might never pick up the skills necessary to act composedly or obediently. Therefore, the most important quality a good teacher must possess is composure. But it's difficult to keep your composure and maintain the same disposition, particularly when the dog is out of control. It's a typical occurrence that if we act like we're beating a dog, it will become aggressive, but if we act lovingly toward it, it will respond positively. Therefore, don't be shocked the next time your dog settles down next to you since they sense your composure. The most important thing to remember is to maintain your composure in any circumstance. Your trainees will eventually begin to reflect on your attitude.

Interaction

Miscommunication between the dogs and the trainer is the main cause of training failure. A trainer must possess great communication skills to effectively carry out the instruction. The only thing standing in the way of a dog's eagerness to learn is a communication gulf between the canine and its owner or trainer. The trainer-student relationship must be very strong to handle a dog correctly. The trainer's effective communication abilities are the only way to accomplish this. To properly train your puppy, you must comprehend its psychology, including its moments of happiness and sadness and its lack of eagerness to obey. Puppies need more attention and care since they are more readily distracted than adult dogs. The more you communicate with the small one, the greater the bridge you can establish. People communicate differently, for example, by using signals or whistles. The goal is to strengthen the link, regardless of its achievement.

Humans can only form strong bonds with one another through spending quality time together; this same notion also applies to the relationship between a dog and its trainer, providing ample opportunity for the development of strong communication. Misunderstandings and confusion are the adversaries of creating a bridge. That's why, while issuing instructions, you should always try to be as explicit as possible. During the first week of training, if you call the dog "come," you shouldn't use "come in" or "come by my side" in the next two and three weeks. These kinds of instructions are unclear. Since dogs aren't as good at using words as humans communicate, try using visual cues instead of spoken commands. Dogs pick up knowledge more quickly from seeing than from hearing. Building communication with dogs can also be greatly aided by being aware of their body language.

To properly educate a puppy or dog, the most crucial traits are calmness and excellent communication. Whether professionally training dogs or managing your own, it will be challenging to train those furry friends if you cannot have a calm relationship with them.

Chapter 4: Training in the Home and Crate

Teaching a new puppy when and where to urinate is one of the hardest things to undertake after adopting them. When you bring your puppy home, you should begin housetraining them. If you have a crate, you will also need to educate your puppy on the proper way to behave when it is expected that he will be in it and that a crate is a happy place.

House Training Advice Here are some pointers for educating your puppy when and where to relieve himself: - Don't forget to take your puppy for regular walks! Due to their small bladders, puppies must have frequent opportunities to urinate to avoid it. As soon as you wake up in the morning, and then again every thirty to sixty minutes during the day, take your puppy for walks.

- Take your puppy to the same site in your yard each time he needs to relieve himself after you've shown him where that is. Your puppy will easily remember that his favorite place to relieve himself is not next to your bed if he is consistently trained to do so outside.

- Have patience. Most dog training experts advise delaying starting your new puppy's formal housetraining until after they are twelve to fourteen weeks old. This is because your puppy will start to have better bladder control by the time he is twelve weeks old, but at eight weeks old, he could not have enough control to be effective in housetraining.

- Never give up! Though your puppy might appear to be struggling with the transition, don't give up! When it comes to house training, your puppy may have good and bad days; he may go back and forth multiple times before he truly grasps the concept. Remember that some puppies can become housebroken in as little as eight to ten weeks, while others require a full year to become truly housetrained. Reward your puppy for good behavior, and don't give up, even if he picks things up quickly or needs more training.

A dog crate is a fantastic tool to help you reach your house training objectives since it gives your dog a limited area to spend alone time and deters accidents, as dogs, by nature, dislike urinating in their dens. Next, we'll talk about crate training advice, but in the meantime, if you can't get your dog a crate, you might consider buying disposable puppy pads. Puppy pads deter your puppy from urinating on your floor by teaching them that there is a designated area inside for them to do so if necessary. To ensure that your puppy associates the act with the same general area, keep the puppy pads next to the door you use to go outdoors for potty training. When you have to leave the house for extended periods and know your puppy will have an accident, puppy pads can also be a useful safety measure.

Crate Instruction

Any puppy and dog owner can benefit from having a thoroughly trained dog in a crate. If he is housebroken, your dog will have his own secure and personal area to sleep or play with his toys. Owners can also benefit greatly from creating because it gives you peace of mind that your dog isn't playing unsupervised (and maybe creating trouble) when you leave the house. Before beginning crate training, you must realize that your dog must associate his crate with a secure and happy place. When you have to clean, entertain guests, or leave the house for a few hours, your puppy should sleep in his crate. When your dog is used as a punishment, it will learn to associate the crate with unpleasant things, making him fear it and hesitant to return to it. Therefore, you should avoid using the crate for punishment.

Crate training might also help you the day you bring your new puppy home, especially if you intend to establish a rule that your dog or puppy is not permitted on the furniture in your house. When your puppy initially comes home, if you let them lie in bed with you, it could quickly become a habit that will be harder to break as your dog ages. When you bring your puppy home, place him in his crate if you do not want him to sleep on your bed. To keep your dog happy and distracted, ensure his kennel has a bed, blankets, and toys (which he is encouraged to chew on). Your puppy may cry or whine a lot the first night in his box after being taken from the litter and brought home with you. If you want your puppy to feel secure resting in his kennel, try placing some of your old, unloved shirts with him. He will be able to smell you.

There are undoubtedly advantages to crate training your dog or a new puppy, but how does one do it?

- Ensure your dog or new puppy has a nice experience when introducing them to their crate. Provide him with his preferred toys or treats to help him feel at ease in the crate. Treats should be used to entice your dog to enter the crate; if you force him inside, he may grow fearful or nervous and refuse to enter on his own.

- Feeding your dog while he is crated is an excellent method to help him positively accept the crate. When you're ready to feed your dog, ask him to go to his crate. Give him his food in his box and keep the door closed until he has eaten all of it. Allow your dog or puppy to go outside once his food is over, and praise him for his good conduct. This will teach him to equate food and praise with his crate.

- When you are home, begin crate training your dog by placing it in the crate for ten minutes. Gradually increase this time to an hour. You can attempt crate-training your dog and then let them leave your house once they are at ease and content in their cage for an extended time.

Puppy Exercises That Take Less Than Ten Minutes

The fly ball exercise is among the top workouts for puppies that take less than ten minutes.

- The brisk 10-minute run,

Three exercises: the smell trail exercise, the low-height jump exercise, and the fetching game

Observe them engaging in play with other animals.

- Commands for obedience

- Advice on obedience training

Dancing with your puppy is a great way to bond.

The Fly-ball drill

Fly-ball training is beneficial for dogs of all ages, including puppies. Dogs that play fly-ball competitively race down a course and hop over obstacles while holding the ball in their mouths. Make sure the ball is not larger than your puppy's mouth when engaging in fly-ball training, and make sure the distance you toss the ball is sufficient for your puppy to run towards and return from. Because fly-ball requires a lot of energy, you should limit it to 10 minutes.

The ten-minute run

Jogging alongside your dog is enjoyable since it doubles as exercise and a multitasking activity. Ensure your dog is wearing a decent leash; it should be long enough to let it run freely without placing undue pressure or strain on it. Puppy jogging improves their strength and endurance. Running for ten minutes should be done in a comfortable environment, and afterward, be sure to offer the pet some water.

The exercise of low-height jumping

Puppies should practice jumping to improve their agility. Because of their small stature, the puppy should not be able to jump higher than their height; this will help them become used to these kinds of exercises more rapidly.

The exercise with the smell trail

Teaching your dog to track and follow various scents at a young age is best. This activity helps increase your dog's mental awareness. Still, it might be a little harder than other exercises because you have to expose your dog to various scents before performing the exercise. While tracking events may not pique the interest of every dog breed, it can be developed. In addition to the smell, you might wish to bury certain objects so your dog can investigate by sniffing them.

To begin with, expose the dog to the fragrance by letting it sniff the object or scent multiple times. Next, place the scent in a designated area and help the animal detect it. Repeat this process 4-5 times before letting the dog detect the scent independently. When the dog recognizes the scent independently without assistance, show it your appreciation and give it a gift.

The game of fetching

Playing fetching games helps your dog learn to detect different objects in diverse environments, so you can play them indoors or outdoors—even when it's pouring. Fitting this 10-minute workout into your hectic schedule is possible, and you can even use a local park. Throw a stick around for your dog to retrieve for the first few minutes. Then, you may become more challenging by hiding the stick or object in the grass, shrubs, or behind trees and watching your dog retrieve it.

Observe them interacting with other animals.

Playing games with other animals is one of the finest ways to exercise your dogs and give them a feeling of community. This is something they naturally like doing. Allowing them to run, jump, and follow the trails of other animals—such as cats and other dogs—will help them gain more strength and agility. However, be cautious about setting boundaries because dogs frequently play with other animals for longer than ten minutes.

Compliance mandates

The fundamentals of teaching your border collie to obey

You must choose your next line of action after deciding on your training timetable. The fundamental commands for obedience training should be sit, come, stay, and down.

Once the border collie has mastered these, you can advance to the harder ones.

Tips for teaching obedience

Say "Come" as soon as your collie approaches you on his initiative, and give him a treat as soon as he complies. After some time, you can move to a different location and give the same order again. If your border collie responds to you, he has most likely mastered the commands "Come" and "Sit."

- Teaching your canine to approach! One of the most crucial commands in border collie obedience training is "Come." This is because, after your dog becomes accustomed to the command, you may safely let him go on off-leash walks in designated areas without worrying that you won't find him. A puppy is usually engaged in something else if he doesn't come when you call for him to, but you can use a treat or toy as a motivator to catch his attention.

Pay attention to the puppy's name, show him the food or toy, reward him when he gets there, and make sure he enjoys the treat by praising him.

Maintain this obedience training as you progressively get farther away from him.

Once the dog begins to accept the instruction, stop giving it rewards.

- How to train your border collie to sit - The steps for both the "Sit" and "Come" training can be repeated. Additionally, you can add some rewards, but make sure the training session is brief. The most challenging aspect of this training is determining why the dog is sitting during the training session. As much as possible, alternate between "Sit" and "Come." When the dog becomes accustomed to the new commands, give him vocal praise. Ensure the dog never sits more than five times in a session or at the same location.

- Teaching your dog to lay down: Your collie can learn the command "Down" in the same manner as they learned the order "Sit." Your dog will typically lay on his stomach if you have him sit and put some food in your fingers and some on the ground in front of the collie. When the food is in the puppy's mouth, you'll see that it wants to stay up, but you may urge him to keep lying down by giving him a gentle pat on the back.

- Teaching your border collie to "Stay": This command, which will help you keep your dog inside when you have guests or want them to remain out of danger, is just as vital as the sit, come, and down commands. It is unrealistic to expect your puppy to pick up this command quickly because he will naturally want to accompany you everywhere.

- Have the collie lie down or sit to begin this obedience training.

- Issue the order to "stay," pairing it with a pointer that indicates the spot you want him to remain in.

As you turn to go, give him the command and gesture to the spot where you want him to stay. Then, stand back and watch him stay.

- Try to extend the time and space as soon as the collie becomes used to this command. He will stay for longer periods.

- Reward the puppy for his cooperation and refrain from punishing him when he disobeys.

While obedience training may not be considered a workout, it is undoubtedly beneficial as it teaches your dog to obey you.

www.ingramcontent.com/pod-product-compliance
Lightning Source LLC
Chambersburg PA
CBHW052134110526
44591CB00012B/1723